Picture Album

Picture Album

poems

A.R. Johnson

GRAYSON BOOKS
West Hartford, Connecticut
graysonbooks.com

For Mary, Mary Margaret, and Pace

Contents

III.

IV.

Beauty and Truth

Now they are brown-eyed Susans,
nodding as I pass and inviting me
to touch their dark, velvety centers
and be smitten by the allure
of their sun-kissed faces.

But they weren't always so comely
and open to pleasure. No,
they began prickly and green
and grew prosaic
before they finally blossomed into poetry.

I.

Maybe

With sore eyes and
certain truth,

this is a time when
we look for angels.

But we each have our own
way of seeing,

and sometimes
certainty divides us

from each other
and from grace.

So maybe we need
to hang on to What If,

and Help Me Understand
You, and Maybe.

Maybe
that's enough.

Uccellini on the Piazza del Popolo

Like a charm of colorful birds dipping and turning against a winter sky,
dozens of children in coats of red and yellow, blue and green,
seen from above and at a distance,

are racing in scattered patterns across the grey piazza.
Their teacher calls, and they come swiftly together to settle on steps,
young fledglings from a flurry of flight alighting.

I hear faint echoes of their laughter and chirping chatter
coming back to me from old walls and empty spaces,
causing me to remember

The black-and-white of ordered nuns in habits rigid with reasons why,
their large, framed faces always too close, seeing into souls,
they said, as my guilt took flight.

Ways the Heart Breaks

Sometimes it breaks along the fine lines
etched by sharp tongues,

or into tiny shards when loss strikes it
like a bullet.

When harbored faults rupture,
it breaks apart like a chiseled stone.

Sometimes it breaks and crumbles into dust
after years of being bloodless,

or it breaks from falling,
a fragile empty vessel, out of love.

And it breaks in two, when nothing
seems to hold together.

But if you're lucky, it will break wide open
to hold the suffering that allows joy.

Unseen

Sometime after the incense and procession,
he slips silently into the pew next to me,
smelling of ashes and carrying a sack made of cloth.

It likely holds all he owns save the clothes he wears.
Maybe he is here to confess, or maybe he is here
because the doors are open and the wind is cold.

His hands, cracked and with creases outlined in black,
are rough and dry when we exchange the peace,
testament to what little of that they have known.

He gingerly takes the prayer book from its rack
and follows the liturgy with eyes that show
his defensiveness as he faces the unfamiliar,

yet he doesn't seem awed or humbled, simply here
among us and unsure exactly for what or why.
And then, before the Eucharist, he disappears,

gone without notice, invisible again,
as he is on the everyday streets.

No

For Bill Knott
1940-2014

Please, no moon tonight.
Let the clouds drape it
with crepe and tattered lace
and hide the light.

Let the stars fade and fall
with no trails, no wishes
made, no difference
who we are at all.

Let there be no more to ponder
than how little we know,
yet how far we wander.

Mourning Clothes

An empty cardinal's nest
perched in the blackened rose canes

like a rakish straw hat
with one feather still clinging to it.

A loose coat of ragged bark
hanging from bent trunk and brittle limbs.

The size of the void left by the sole
of a worn-out work boot in the frozen mud.

Icicles dangling like spangly earrings
from the rusted gutter rim,

and the pale and paper-thin skin of frost
stretched over the bare bones of morning.

This is how we try on death
every winter.

Remember

In a flurry of flutters and stops,
her bony blue hands, in her lap
and out, mix invisible ingredients,
turning them over and over
between twisted fingers
that want to fly away.

She could once make a crust so fragile
and perfect the only way to know
was to see it crumble and taste
its sweetness and remember
her grafted apple trees and
how the limbs bowed down with grace
and bore us fruit to slice so thin
that the light could almost pass through.

Bella Luna

The moon wears a veil over her face
and is all the more alluring for it,
playing a peek-a-boo game with lace
the clouds weave and the wind lifts.

She shows herself like this tonight
in a slow reveal that's sometimes new
and every time luminous and light,
often all it takes to madden we who

pay her close attention and heed
her pull, give in to stunning beauty,
the undeniable attraction, and the need
to be immersed in something unearthly.

Proof

Archer and bull, chained maiden and the bearer of water,
a crab, a compass, and the southern cross.
The night sky's intricate lacework is woven
in patterns of unknowable time and distance,

so we give them the names of forms we know.
I look up at them and only now can see
the light of suns thousands of millennia past.
And here in smallness, centered on myself,

I look for proof I am not meant to find,
reach for hands I cannot seem to grasp.
and I am cold, and so I pull a blanket closer,
seeking comfort from a weaver unknown.

La Lumiere

He is thin and careworn,
austere and elegantly frayed,
sitting in a bare wooden chair,
its frame a match of his own.

He has much to teach us,
taking a thin slice of life
and holding it up to light,
giving it transparency.

We have much to learn
in the dark thicket
of human trial and error,
a place plagued with blindness.

He rises to address us,
to question our assumptions
and lay claim to holes in our faith.
We must light a candle.

What the Squirrel Knows

In a nest tucked in tendrils,
promise is broken
by the jackhammer bill of a jay
as a red-tail sets off a shrill alarm
that ruptures silence
and a fast-forward squirrel
goes suddenly still, knowing
how the sky might strike
again, how talons grip and tear,
how the shell of a skull
cracks like the perfect blue egg
tucked in the tendrils.

Denier's Lament

The days are warmer than the former ones,
    so when the storms come
        the rain that once danced a tin-roof tango
           pounds out a fierce flamenco,
        wind that once whispered now roars its threats,
           and summer's heat lightning gives way to epithets
              of hellfire and brimstone.

At water's edge, the sea rises up and its waves take down homes,
    and in the parched center, drought moves in and stays,
        while the polar ice melts and runs away.
Too late to just say I'm sorry, I was wrong,
    too soon to give up and say it's already gone.

Never-Ending

Start in mountains so high
they nearly touch the moon,
and then come down
into the mother valley
like a quiet leaf lifted
by a loud stream
and made to go on,
to spin in eddies,
move across ragged rocks
and around smooth stones,
to pass over shallows
and through deep waters,
to undertake bridges,
and finally fall
into the bottomless black
of a pool that gathers
with collected calm and
then flows again, true
in a trace never-ending.

Stopped Short

"It's as large as life and twice as natural"
—*Lewis Carroll,* Through the Looking-Glass and What Alice
Found There

When a barred owl flew hard against a window and fell
onto the soft cushion of a chair beneath, I thought
I had encountered the moment when death strikes.

Its unblinking eyes stared up at me, but it was not
death's face; it was a misguided creature,
tricked by reflected sky and human invention.

In a freeze-frame closeup, here was perfected handiwork:
the exquisitely colored feather coat, layered and fine,
awkwardly folded wings still beautiful in their stillness,
and the banded, barreled chest moving in rapid rhythm.

"Think twice about a trip through the looking glass,"
it seemed to say to me. "You may become nothing more
than a tuft of down and a dun-colored smudge on the windowpane,
reflection and reality stopping you short." And then it flew away.

Belief

"What isn't there has a presence, like the absence of light."
—Margaret Atwood

There is the wind with its hand
in the leaves and on my cheek,
the dead or dying stars with pure light
a thousand years in coming,
and the proof of a rabbit's ragged foot
in the freshly fallen snow.
They are how I can believe
without knowing.

Procession

An old man wearing a faded, plaid cap,
stoop-shouldered and bent forward at the waist,

with his head down but with eyes focused
on what's to come, moves along our street,

pulling his white-muzzled and cloudy-eyed
golden retriever in a homemade wooden wagon.

The dog sits facing forward, its head also bowed,
regal and yet a little forlorn, resigned to going slow.

In front of the man dances a much younger dog,
it, too, a golden, maybe a descendant, maybe

just a replica to preserve the knowing and the love.
They move in a solemn, sweet procession

along a determined and well-traveled path,
age overtaking them but the road still ahead.

Belle

The bell of her clarinet moves in a repeating arc
that reaches to a cloudless French Quarter sky

and dips back toward the cobbled street still damp
from a desultory morning sweep of last night's leavings.
Her eyes are closed, her face glistens black and beatific,

and she taps time with the thrust of powerful legs, close
to dance in a folding chair. She owns this corner,
the locals say, and most days she and her trio are here

to make music so pure it pours from her like light and heat
and sometimes like a rare cool breeze. We listen.

Into a Circle

A young girl stands on the Minnesota prairie,
looks at the line between heaven and earth,
and moves toward it into a circle that she fills
with what she thinks she wants,
and when she grows to be a woman,
what she knows.
She pulls it tight around her and is content
with all it holds and whom,
at first being happy, and then telling herself
stories about being happy.
And as the years go by,
the circle becomes smaller and smaller
until it is a single point on a line
that circumscribes eternity.

Itasca

They stand in wooded rows,
aligned as pews but closer to heaven.
They are elders, ringed with the truth
of a thousand seasons,
come together in a place where a river is born
and flows across miles and down mountains
from a stream to the sea.

In autumn, they cast off their raiment
to make the muffled paths to peace.
They whisper in summer from on high
the calming balm of Gilead,
at Preachers Grove, offer shelter and reprieve,
and in winter lead us here to grieve.

In My Silence

For Radford Brooks
1951-1994

There, on the parapet, was a man
waiting to jump.
I could see him from the street below.
I knew him. He was my friend.

In a voice I didn't hear,
he called to me
to come and pull him back.
And in my silence, I called him to jump.

And he did.

Red Sky at Morning

"It's a poet's sky," someone said,
though it could be anyone's, really.

It has hallelujah and glory in it,
but it also has the promise of rain.

Rain of trouble, rain of riches. Who knows?
Maybe it is a poem, with beauty in the form,

rhythm in the coming of another day,
music in the breaks through which light appears,

meter in the systematic pattern of dark and dawn,
and meaning in seeing it all again this morning.

Going Home

The muffled drumming of apples falling
marks the cadence of the days,
an irregular rhythm of the fruits of his labor
going to ground at season's end.

With the damp chill settling in,
the migrant worker remembers spring and seedlings
and the promise of blossoms,
holds a non-believer's faith in a certain cycle.

He thinks about his wife and their casita, about her rosary,
about how she believes divine favor will protect him
from these chills and fever and gasping for air,
from the day when his pay won't come.

And so he rises from his hard bed and from under
the thin blanket in a shack at the edge of the trees
to reach his hands toward heaven one more time,
to ask for strength, for grace.

To the Garden

For Carolyn Donnet
1926 – 2020

After Jane Kenyon

Let the warmer days and softer sun come,
And let me go to the garden.
Let the earth turn, let seeds fall,
the rains come, and life be lifted to light.
Let the tended canes bear berries
to ripen as certain summer comes.

Let the leaves stir and turn,
the days shorten, the nights be quicker to fall.
Let a sharper wind blow and snow
put a first coat on the hills' cold shoulders.
Let swift birds turn south, the mouth
of the creek crust over, ice and stillness come.

Let the paths I made, the work of my hands,
comfort the steps of those who follow
as I lie down for the long winter
and, safely sheltered, see evening come.
Let rest come, then let love stay,
and let me now gently go.

II.

Crow

Solemn, in your suit of soot,
as a judge, you cast a gimlet eye
over the common robin,
find it inadequate,
and declare it dismissed.
Pausing, you caw,
then claw at your tilted head
like a sleek yet flea-bitten cat,
giving in to the pleasure,
your dignity scratched.

Feeling Empty

She had a golden crown,
that perfectly firm bottom,
always needed buttering up
when she called for her honey.
Flaky as could be,
she would lose her lightness
if I weren't gentle.
I couldn't get enough of her,
but she rose one morning
too hot to handle,
and was gone,
leaving me feeling empty.

Scarecrow Gotta Dance

The ghost of the garden
has a gig in a fallow field,

rattles the sentry
and raises the dead cornstalks,

strums sagging strings
that once held tomato vines,

blows a mean cadenza
on an empty horn of plenty,

and turns hollowed gourds
into a pair of maracas,

making all manner of music
In the moonlight.

Truce

Overseen by the clarity of a rain-scoured sky,
these two tow-headed boys are now a far cry
from the ones sent out into the steamy heat
of an afternoon left to them by the retreat
of a sudden summer storm. It lashed
the tin roof and weeping willow and crashed
into the still surface of the pond and then
moved on as quickly as it came to upend
and soak the nearly dry and dingy clothes hung
on lines behind a neighbor's farmhouse. Among
the hardscrabble hollows partly cleared of trees,
it left behind just a whiff of a cooler breeze,
and a usually placid creek now filled with babble
and plash, the one where the boys do battle
on its slippery banks. Waving sticks as swords,
they unite to fight the marauding hordes
that invaded when their long afternoon nap,
brought on by black clouds, left wide gaps
in defenses and laid open the field of battle.
They fling insults, mud, and small stones, rattle
their sassafras sabers against faded overalls
but declare a truce when their mother calls.

Read to Me

We went so many places, you and I,
Riding there on the sound of my voice.
You stayed close by my side
Night after night as we sailed the wide
And wordy seas and found our way
Back home at end of story, end of day.
After doing that over many years,
Listening, learning, overcoming fears,
You one day left for your own shores,
Opening to life, closing familiar doors.

The Clock's Face

Has guilt
written all over it.

Guilty of reminding me
how late it is,

Guilty of having fast hands
with no second thoughts,

Of triggering alarms,
ticking me off.

Guilty of running in circles
just to pass the time.

But it winds up being as honest
as the day is long.

Love's on It

An Ode to Form in 14 Lines

I am so in love with how you're made,
my devotion will surely never fade.
Adore your form, can't resist your lines,
I scan your length, and you hypnotize

With a song that calls me back for more,
tight stanzas that entrance this troubadour.
For you, my love, I am bicker free,
by the meter or the foot, we so agree.

Yet there are times you must stand apart,
separated by spaces, the conventions of art,
when rules apply and measures are taken,
no way for something new to awaken,

So I am given this and one more line
to complete my formulaic valentine.

Cheers

Here's to the jiggered gin
and to the crested crystal in which it's poured.
Let's toast the Hinckley and this morning's win,
to Daddy's toy, polished and snugly moored.

Here's to black silken sheaths and risqué skirts
that show well-tanned legs and firm young thigh,
to freshly laundered Turnbull & Asher shirts
with no concern; the market's still high.

Let's drink to Cole Porter and the Barrymores,
to the idea of Fitzgerald despite his failures,
to surreptitious sex with paramours
and jukey jazz with syncopated measures.

But not to the creep of too-early light
around the damask curtain,
and tomorrow's inevitable petty fight
that will leave us shaken and uncertain

until the ritual occasion
of gathering to wash away our sin,
not because of any religious persuasion,
but with a toast to the jiggered gin.

Gobsmacked

Bushwhacked, body-slammed,
dope-slapped and
hornswoggled.

T-boned, blind-sided,
cold-cocked and
addlepated.

Browbeaten, humiliated,
sucker-punched and
eviscerated.

Hogtied, hung up,
smacked down and
screwed over.

But I'm all right now.

Second-Hand Rose

A past-its-prime, slip-covered sofa
with soft arms and arched back,
padding in all the right places,
curves that beckon,
is being hauled down the Interstate
in a flat-bed trailer, out in the open,
all by itself and finally going places,
caught up in something unexpected
and ready to take on somebody new.

Nashvillanelle

I count on my fingers, so I can't pick the banjo,
can't play the fiddle or strum a Gibson guitar,
but I'm headed to Nashville to play Music Row.

I'll take my big hat (this ain't my first rodeo),
and spend every night in a honky-tonk bar.
I count on my fingers, so I can't pick the banjo.

Got some gator boots with silver-tipped toes,
the drunks will all tell me I'm bound to go far.
I'm headed to Nashville to play Music Row.

I'll be bigger than Waylon, yodel like Bill Monroe,
have fans that wear tank tops, a shiny Cadillac car.
But I count on my fingers, so I can't pick the banjo.

Singin' on the road again, goin' where tour buses go,
we'll smoke weed like Willie and pass a Mason jar.
I'm headed to Nashville to play Music Row.

Yeah, I'm flat broke, the rent's due; it's time to go
on down to Music City, gonna be an Opry star.
I count on my fingers, so I can't pick the banjo,
but I'm headed to Nashville to play Music Row.

III.

One Morning This Spring

The air is a bit softer, and the sun
rises over the tree line a little earlier
when I step outside to feed the bluebirds I'm courting,
startle a thieving squirrel, and survey the mackerel sky.

A tattered blanket of rust and dun
is rolled to the foot of a wintered-over flower bed,
and the smothered survivors are laid bare
to the breaking rays of new heat in a thinner sky.

It's a morning sun now capable of stirring nascent life,
the mother's hand on a restless but still sleepy newborn,
and then it moves on to vernal days in other places
already awake and waiting.

Late December

If this were a day in August,
one when the air is heavy and still,
the fields sated with blossoms and shaggy
with unkempt hay, everything lush and lazy,
full of sunshine and finally ripe,
there would be this present,
and time seemingly without end to savor it.
But it is instead a day in late December
when the city air is raw and thin, stripped
of all it held and left with the smell of poverty,
trees like skeletons, scratching at the sky,
streetlights a row of moons in the dim afternoon,
nothing expectant, everything drawn in and down.

Letting Go

After the deep sleep of a snow-drifted winter,
their new growth and green of last spring,
and the shade they spread this summer,
it's autumn, and the oak trees in the backyard
got rhythm, make percussive music, and let go.
Their fusillade starts us awake
on one of the dun days when the fissures
of our growing apart are patched
and prettied up, in the dark before
the toaster pops, a screen door slaps,
and the old blue Buick growls
in the chilly air of morning
in this time before we, too, let go.

Regrets Only

In the space between sunshine and dark,
the whites of blossoms that were here,
but overlooked and nearly invisible, appear
as dazzling points of light and so mark
the passing of another day spent
blindly unaware of all that was sent
to us and missed while we tallied our debts
and costs with nothing to save but regrets.

Winter's Dark

These bare branches, now without the seasonal players
that put on a sold-out show in gold and crimson costumes,
are the flies and rigging where a feathery chorus sings.

The rustle of the wind's applause in the halls below is muffled,
for the songs are hymns of mourning; the light of day is dying.
But while still here, reflecting off the water, slanted on the land,

it casts shadows to remind us of how like ourselves we are,
even as the changes come, even when we are stretched so thin,
putting one foot in front of the other, going toward winter's dark.

After the Rain

Before birds reappear from their secret shelter
to speak to us harshly or sing something sweet,
before the screen-door slams, children go out to play,
and the dogs catch a new scent worth barking about,
in the stillness framed by the soft sounds
of beads falling in strands from limbs and leaves,
a breeze stirs the skirts of the willow,
and light streams between a few loitering clouds
to grace this place, now somehow sacred.

Snow Melts into Music

—Title from John Muir

The first hot licks
of the morning sun
set up a rhythm
that is the music
of improvisation,
the score from sound
and silence, a steady
line of time and tempo,
the giving way
to a meandering riff.
Listen closely. The god
of jazz is in the refrain.

Just Now

Give us this grey workday in early winter
when the damp, chill air is close around,
not a blazing-bright summer Saturday,
all possibility and blue-sky high, but instead
a day with limits and circumscribed horizon,
one like collected calm water–reflecting,
not rushed–to show there is sanctity
in knowing how to be still,
believing that just now is enough.

Past the Dark

After I put a fresh coat of thin white paint
on the old weather-worn fence in a corner
of our backyard, the pocket that was shadows
and most days forgotten comes back to life.

The withered vines I trimmed and left where they fell
are now the ruffle on the hem of a box-pleated skirt.
Ragged shrubs suddenly need a haircut,
and like teenagers trying to escape a small town,
the limbs of skinny saplings are edging over the line.

The nodding hydrangeas hang their heavy heads over
patches of grass laced with light in the late afternoon,
and something that was lost has reasserted itself
so I can see past the dark.

Thinking of You

After Charles Simic

Every morning now we awake thinking of you,
hoping you're only a few days away, as we
pull on our grey winter coats once again

and look forward to seeing you arrive, all dazzling
in bright pinks and purples, the occasional red,
that pale green that makes you look so young.

Most of your finery will be floral, the de rigueur
buds and splashy blossoms, but there will also be
streaks of gold, ochre, and indigo mixed in,

and the stippled dots of white in a new pattern
on the background of nubby brown and straw,
a light wrap to drape around cold shoulders.

October

I need to drink in this day
      as a single, perfect draught of autumn

until I know it as well as I know my lover
      but not so well that I take it for granted.

I need to see copper and gold spilling into the sky,
      filling the space between summer and the long night.

I need to feel air that has lost its heavy hand
      and taken on a light touch, barely brushing my cheek.

I need to squint into the crystalline sunlight
      that brings a glimpse of clarity

and yet doesn't reveal anything that matters more
      than the smell of wood smoke and the snap of a football.

Let It Snow

In the short days and long shadows at the end
of a tired old year, let something like snow fall,

and let it soften the hard edges, hide
the pieces that are pulled apart and broken.

Use it as comfort on a cold day, as cover
for all the imperfection that can't be fixed.

And let go of the guilt and the sorrow,
let the wind take the woe and the worry,

but hang on to hope and healing, the hands
reaching out to you, all that gives you peace.

Do-si-do

I head out across the melting snow,
        putting one foot in a barren patch
        of brown and still-frozen ground,
        hopping on the other
to the left
        and then back
                to the right
        to avoid an icy rivulet
          r
        u
         n
           n
          i
            n
             g
      a
       zig-
        zag
      course.

With a rhythm
        set by the shape
        of the earth's rocks and ridges,
I dance to steps
        called by the sun.

IV.

At the End

The boy who once herded cows from the woods at the far end of the pasture is now an old man easing himself into his chair, closing his eyes to relive a cold, grey morning in his childhood. He's back watching himself crawl from under a ragged quilt, pull on his overalls, and walk into the mist and the hollows as daylight comes and forms take shape along the ridgetops.

Back walking in soft, black earth behind an old brown mule, calling gee and haw as the plow puts furrows in the brow of a steep hillside, back walking home to a farmyard as full with people as on a Sunday when ice cream got cranked, but so hushed he could hear the noise of wind stirring leaves as he stopped to study the downcast eyes and nervous looks on the faces of men gathered on the porch.

Back staring for one last time at the ashen face and closed eyes of his father, lying rigid in a wooden box at the front of their one-room country church, its wide-plank floors scrubbed clean, and the smell of gathered-up flowers reminding him of last Easter's service and the sermon about life everlasting.

Just Before Blood Cries Out from the Ground

And Cain said to Abel, "Let's go out to the field."
—The Book of Genesis

Two brothers who have grown to hate each other
as much as they have come to distrust their own land
stand in a partly plowed field beside an old Farmall,
the tractor's crankcase covered with a caul of dirty oil.
There is the smell of hot machinery and turned dirt,
the metallic ticking of the cooling motor, and a swarm
of sweat bees. Around the men lies the hollow
of their worn-out farm, mostly hillsides and ridgetops
with a few flat places where five generations
scratched out seed rows and what passed for a living.

The men are hard and thin, their overalls hang on them
like rags on a scarecrow, and their feed-store caps with arched bills
darken faces as cracked and brown as their work boots.
The older brother spits a fat tobacco stream onto the hay stubble
beside his brother's feet, then bends to tighten the hex-headed oil plug.
Goddamn it, Floyd, you let it get that low again I'll whip your ass.

The younger one opens a toolbox their father made, fastened
below the tractor seat with strips of riveted tin, rusted out now
like the plow, one more thing that can't be sold to try to satisfy the bank.
He feels the hard, true implements of work: the jaws of a pair of pliers,
the wire cutters' bite, the jagged teeth of the hacksaw,
and the handle of a ballpeen hammer.

As the love of their mother hangs above them and the hopes
of their father lie with him in a narrow plot behind the church,
yellowjackets whine and settle, grackles burst from a sour gum,
and the hammer is raised to the sun.

Morning Unbroken

My grandmother folds flour and buttermilk with certain wisdom,
her cupped hands veined and wrinkled but still strong.
The cook stove's wood-smoke drifts from the stacked-stone chimney
and settles to the ground, and a ragged blanket of fog
covers alfalfa and timothy in the meadow.

In the spreading dawn, a hawk hunts over the back pasture
where rabbits build nests in the hay fields, a Blue Racer
leaves its initials in the dusty road to the barn,
and crawdads move along the muddy creek bottom,
its surface clouded over by a swarm of minnows and mayflies.

Later my grandfather will walk behind his mules
and squint down the straight row he sees before it's ever plowed.
He will call to the pair to pull and strain, do the necessary work,
and move his feet and shift his weight to walk on sudden hills,
then make another turn.

Picture Album

Aunt Elsa died yesterday, and I can't help but think about her face,
floating just above the car's rolled-down window glass, that day
they moved her from her old homeplace to somewhere in Florida.

She was bundled into the backseat of her lawyer son's Chevrolet,
her head's white crown like a fistful of bloomed-out honeysuckle
as she twisted her neck and turned to look back one last time.

You could have about read a book in the lines of her face,
the sweet-sad story of a life in the hollows of a threadbare farm.
I imagine the pictures her cloudy old eyes must have taken,
crimped at the corners by folds and crows' feet, blurred by tears,
but wide open and fixed on a place growing smaller, then gone.

On the Front Porch of a Shack Built for Tenant Farmers

Great wings of dust dotted with grasshoppers
fan out on either side of a fast-moving pickup
parting the bushy crown of the ridgetop across the hollow.
The fierce sun, slung low, turns the settling haze gold,
and there's a thrumming in the coming night air,
the Pennyroyal summer dusk growing louder
with the catcalls of katydids and crickets.

A man as faded and worn as his overalls
lights a Lucky Strike, settles into a cane-bottomed chair,
and leans back to tilt it off the dusty, rutted porch planks.
He breathes out a stream of smoke and hears his wife
close their bedroom door. He pushes back his frayed-bill cap
and looks across to the county road as the dark comes on,
watching one of her lovers floor his truck,
stirring up gravel and the start of another fight.

He's thinking maybe this time there's no fight left,
just a kind of void and distance
that mimics the space between his place and the road,
but there's no scent of supper on the stove, none
of his work clothes on the line strung behind the house,
and every chance the door that she closed she locked.

A Better View

The restless woman pulls her pruning shears from the drawer
and unwraps them, removes the linseed-oil-soaked cloth
that smells of work long done.

She walks with purpose from the kitchen to the front porch
that's shaded by a scrim of clematis and morning glory
and stretches as far as the stiffness of age will allow
to trim a better view to the highway beyond the yard.

But she stops when she sees a nest tightly formed
among the tendrils and leaves, filled with hatchlings
that ceaselessly open and close their beaks,
make tiny mewing sounds, and turn their still-damp heads
always upward, staring with eyes not yet formed.

The promise of freedom songs and flying away, she decides,
is worth more than the small world she's trying to see.

Last Turn

With ragged breath, the wind sings
in a soft, high tenor.
The dying sun shadows the tall grasses
as its light gives way to the rising
of a pale, half-made moon.

In the field at the edge of the woods,
the farmer makes a last turn with his team
and heads toward the barn and home.
He looks back to take a measure of work done
and makes the calling, low-voiced sounds
that always settle his horses and himself.

When he finishes his chores, dusk
will be crossing the worn-down side yard.
No light will show in the windows,
and the kitchen door will be a shadow
in the fading outline of the house he built
three decades before his wife died.

He will enter it without pause and with purpose,
intending to always live here like this
in the circle of sowing and reaping, in a dance
with his land and the weather called by the sun,
even as his back and his bones tell him
someday this sweet music will end.

Guideposts

When the fire is low and the moon is down,
I think of the blind farmer,
his world through a tunnel dimmed to dark
but his spirit a light everlasting.

I see his wrinkled, brown face and lopsided smile,
his strong, thick hands flicking his stick
that keeps him from tripping
as he uses his feet to read the ground and listens
to twigs and leaves and brush, in broad day nocturnal.

There is a map fixed in his mind of the fields and barns,
the orchard and the creek bed,
and across it run the lines that are his highways:
fence posts as guideposts, touched and true.
Slow he goes, with patience that had to be learned
and at a pace that allows him to sense more than we see.

Though lost and mourned are the flash of a fish in the stream,
the glint of sun on snow, the feathery tips of pines at dusk,
the faces of his children, he still knows them by scent or sound
and what he remembers.

He says he believes in the Holy Ghost.
It taps him on the shoulder and says "Go there."
And he follows.

Here Is the Peace

A maple tree in autumn
with its crown
a sun-stoked fire,
the evening coming down
behind it, the spent fields
folded over themselves,
and rattling blackbirds
going to roost.
Here is the peace
of an ending.

Acknowledgments

"Guideposts" appeared in *The Cortland Review*, under the title "The Blind Farmer."

"The Clock's Face" was published in the *Wisconsin Review*.

"Uccellini on the Piazza del Popolo," "Mourning Clothes," "Just Before Blood Cries Out from the Ground," and "Picture Album" were published in *Connecticut River Review*.

About the Author

A.R. Johnson grew up spending weekends and summers at his family's farm in Tennessee, and his career has been in business and non-profit leadership. He was an invited contributor to the Sewanee Writers' Conference from 2012 to 2019, and his poems have appeared in *The Cortland Review, Wisconsin Review, Connecticut River Review, The New York Times*, and other publications.

www.ingramcontent.com/pod-product-compliance
Lightning Source LLC
Chambersburg PA
CBHW051234120626
46547CB00013B/1645